Who Will Buy My Posies

poems by

Carol Siemering

Finishing Line Press
Georgetown, Kentucky

Who Will Buy My Posies

ACKNOWLEDGMENTS

The title of this book *Who'll Buy My Posies* comes from a round I learned in
1961, when I was eighteen and living in an international community of women,
The Grail. It was there that I learned about women's power, sensitivity, wisdom,
creativity and connection to the Sacred. It was there I learned about women's
capacity to transform themselves and the world. This book's poems, written
over the many years since then, are all about women: women real and imagined,
women singly and women together.

As the theme of this chapbook is all about women, I would first like to acknowledge
all the extraordinary women who have been in my life. A special thanks to my
daughters, Christina and Ana; two of the most amazing women I know. I would
like to give a shout out to all the wonderful poetry workshop facilitators and
workshop mates who have been partners and an inspiration to me in my long
journey as a poet. Thanks too, to Elizabeth Baubach for her technical help in
getting the manuscript ready.

Publisher: Leah Huete de Maines
Editor: Christen Kincaid
Cover Art: Victor Gabriel Gilbert, *Flower Seller in front of the Madeleine Church*
Author Photo: Ana Siemering
Cover Design: Carol Siemering

Order online: www.finishinglinepress.com
also available on amazon.com

Author inquiries and mail orders:
Finishing Line Press
PO Box 1626
Georgetown, Kentucky 40324
USA

Contents

Moon Chant

Let the green snake creep
the dragonfly flit
with its sheer veined wings
its needle-nose blade
against the warm July wind.
Let them go where they will
in the plum night.

I view all as a daughter
of the Tribe of the Old Irish
who feared neither flying
nor crawling thing
who placed the Great Stones

on the circle ridge
burrowed cool paths
to earthen caves.

The eyes of my Family
saw the light
that hides between the stars
and their feet danced
Meter and Rhyme into being

and I
I know all life is glowing
florescent
sharp-shining
in the glen.

Bonita Springs

Annie takes a long drag on her cigarette.
She is impatient for something to happen.
Anything.
The ash glows.

And though she has heard
that no one walks
into the same stream twice
she has somehow found
over and over
the same spot
with its gray pebbles and stones.

Lines creep on her face
even as she sits inhaling.
Her fingers arthritically curl
(ever so slightly).

Yesterday she was ten
twenty-four
fifty-eight.
And whatever (whoever) it was
that was supposed to transform her
mysteriously like a Eucharist host—
it hasn't happened.
She stubs the butt
into the already full ashtray.
The traffic outside the lanai
rolls on mindlessly—
people going to and from
the shore
where today
the sky and water
have no distinguishable line.

Miss Make-up

rides my bus.
At first I found her garish
almost impossible,
a living caricature,
if she'd done herself up in crayons.

Tripled black eyebrows,
lipstick tracing lips
only her purple-shadowed eyes had seen,
blush that no underbelly of a robin
ever equaled,
her dyed yellow hair
a stiff straw halo to her head.

She wears strong high platformed heels,
wraps herself in leopard in the winter.
Slim silver threads wander thru
her lighter garbs.
Clothes from other people's yesteryears.

But I've come to find her
beautiful,
adventurous,
daring.

I wait to see what purse she'll clutch,
with what wonderful flair
she'll flaunt today, her bold bounty.
Perhaps a rhinestone bracelet,
a Russian shawl,
a lace slip hanging inches from her skirt.

And as I sit here
amid the greys, the beiges,
the tired sleepy eyes,
I've come to see the make-up,
like the rest,
is not a mask

but an illumination!
a glowing!
and I bask in its light.

Lounsbury's

In the early 50's, on hot summer's days,
Tommy, Nancy and I would walk three miles to get there—
our rough towels rolled under our arms,
five cents for a soda, another five for walking in.
Tommy would sneak in
over the cliff of glistening rocks
to save his nickel for a candy bar.

It was a small lake the teenagers
would try to swim across
before the lifeguards saw them,
whistled them back.
We could swim some, in our own
awkward, untaught way.
No board, we would dive from
someone's cupped intertwined hands.

A friendly older boy offered his to me.
I climbed and dove, climbed and dove
and then his hand was inside my bathing suit…
"down there".
I simply walked out, the small waves lapping my waist.
Never said a word to anyone. You didn't in those days.
Never went in again if he was in the water.

Once, in our sixties,
lying on my sister's bed,
cancer fisting her lungs,
I asked her if it had happened to her.
What?! No. Never.
Huh, I mumbled,
perplexed but glad.

in '58, they built a municipal pool at Depew Park,
with clear, chlorinated water.
We went there after that.

Karaoke

When we were kids
Ruth (my mom)
would whisk us to musty bars
she   her   girlfriends   lapping beers
a feast of cokes and fries for us.
My sister and I would saddle up to the piano at Nino's
croon the latest songs.

She died at 53.
The certificate said cirrhosis
but it really was death by broken dreams.
She never met Ana her granddaughter
a princess of a thing
blonde hair running like a river
always polite   appropriate
not one to make a scene.

Ana says Mom   *Dickey's in town*
you should come down to The Place—
a bar down "the Lake" filled with young guys
baseball hats on backwards
a Barbie who did not age with grace
a character from 'The Sopranos"
a man in an impeccable suit
whose delivery by forceps
apparently didn't go too well
and a room full of regular folks
out for a Friday   being Frank   being Patsy.

She grabs the mike   drapes the wire just so
sits herself casually on the stool
leg over leg
and belts it out.
The crowd cheers and claps.

Now   they don't talk much about the Dead
coming back to barrooms
but I believe that somewhere
smoke in smoke   Ruth is here
smiling her butt off.

Sarah Beth is fourteen today

The hair on her skin is downy
but on her head it is impossibly red—

The color of hardwood.
Still   it is as soft and slippery as water.
She's put it up with long steel pins.
Small medusan snakes
escape their stays.

Mother died when her sister was born.
Mother with her brown eyes
sunlight flecks slivered near the center
whose   eyes were warm pools.

I am a young lady now
my neckline is dropped   a little
my petticoats touched with lace.
My sister plays with her ragdoll.
Nanny sits with her   sewing a scene and
Cook's hands are full of flour.

Mother would have known
the importance of this day.

Father steps into the room
begging her pardon.
He has something in his hand
wrapped in soft tissue.
"For you," he says shyly and leaves.

It is a brooch such as a lady would wear
complex and filigreed
And the stone?
The stone is brown
brown with golden flecks
golden flecks swimming
in a dark warm pool.

Holly

They stand in the kitchen,
her head level with
the hip of her mother
whose apron is flecked
with blue forget-me-nots.
Their golden centers,
if you stare hard and long enough,
will take you to the place
where you are looking at yourself
looking at yourself
looking at yourself—
a backward periscope.

Bananas sit in a wooden bowl
on the oak table.
They are as solid as canes.
She peels them one strip at a time,
revealing underneath a flesh
of exactly the same form
but soft and malleable.

They will make a sweet
bread from them
tossing in walnuts
while her father stands
against a porch pillar
searching the sky
for wandering geese.

The Grail

written after an anniversary gathering at Grailville in the 70's

we sisters of the Cup
  together
in sun-day
  Bread and song
the longing back
and new again

blue sky and broad field
 that brings
the frightened secret
 nights of us
  to light
  to share
  to trust…

see, we have all known
  pain
lain lonesome
 in its arms
it is here we meet—
as if each separate
  grain unique
  and yet together
   more—
sand that fill the shore

do you see then
this kingdom here
  built upon these sands
  rising from them
  challenging the ocean
as it stands
  and fades
all impermanence.

we too shift
  are drawn in
  touched and turned
 spat out perhaps

churned by roiling water
owned by it
freed from it

yet still, (oh wonder!)
somehow maintain
  this kingdom's
fluid solid base—
face to face
  and outward turning—
gathered and begotten
  at the same time

we sing and pray
  work, play
drink, wish merry
feel weak and strong
wear worker's boot's
  and aprons

are women
  oh, are women
touched and touching
  sands together—
an uncertain shore
but more…

yes more!

Ah, Noreen

It was just a small store
on a small street in a small town
in New Hampshire.

And there you were

everywhere I looked—
the exquisite handmade pewter jewelry,
the wool spun floppy hats—
with their knitted blooms,
the hand-crafted soaps,
the odd beads and fixings
and oh yes, those tablecloths
(from France or Italy or wherever)
that you loved so much.
I could see the yellow print one
that covered that Arthurian table of yours,
I could see your yellow dishes,
the purple glasses,
hear the witty dialog that rang
around it.

And when I told the owner
how wonderful her store was
and she launched into a tale of
how she was a potter
and couldn't pot because it was too cold,
and whoever partnered her had left
and how she would probably
have to sell the store…
I could see your eyebrows rise
at how "inappropriate" it was
for her to spew all that.

And there in that little remote store
I somehow felt so unexpectedly, so keenly
the scrape of that place you held inside of me.
Ah, my dear Noreen,
I felt so simply and so powerfully
my terrible loss.

A Little Supper Before Singing

Early September
me   (up to that point) on a fat-free diet
Laura   raised "down South."

Tomatoes from her garden
crayola red and green

Perrier   water in wine glasses
the red— still sun-warm
a drizzle of balsamic vinegar
a slide of extra virgin olive oil

the green— "fried the way
my grandma made them"
a silk batter of cornmeal and flour
oil   just-right-smokin-hot
gold crumbs glistening.

We ate and ate and ate—
our forks smacking our plates
salt stinging our lips
teeth and tongue in a revel of chew and taste

and somehow got
uncontrollably   absolutely   deliriously
drunk   could hardly stand.

At madrigals
we were kindergarten-giddy
couldn't hold the line of music.
We were embarrassing ourselves.

We were a little in love.

We were the crackling oil
the funky earth
the ripe and unripe fruit
set to pleasure
We were blissed and blessed
red and green tomato high!

Peggy

In the end it was a deer tick that got her.
She began to diminish bit by bit.

Best Personality,
Most Popular—
class of '61.
She didn't come to our 50th reunion because
she didn't want to come in a wheelchair.
(She'd been emcee at all the others.)

She had been a light glowing,
She had been a friend to all.
She had been all that.
And more.

I had to leave right after the wake on Thursday—
103 temperature riding the Greyhound bus
back to Boston,
ended up in the hospital, sick with grief,
missed the granddaughters
doing Irish step dancing—
their flying feet
drying the tears
of those who gathered
after the funeral.

What They Left Out of Luke 10: 38-42

Martha was worn out.
Mary with her smooth olive skin
her kohl-lined eyes
still sitting at the Rabbi's feet—

Martha had ground the wheat
pat it into flat loaves, baked it,
and Mary sat.

Martha spit the meat,
poured their very best wine from the wine skins,
and Mary gazing upward
gathered her knees in her silky arms.

When the men were done,
the scraps of lamb, of bulgur,
the wooden dishes
were gathered by Martha.
Mary swung her scented hair
to the other side and the men smiled.

Martha turned to Jesus (known in these parts
for his wisdom, his miracles,
his raising their brother from the dead)
and said "Is this fair? I do all the work while she sits?"

Jesus answered (and this what Luke wrote)
"Dear Martha don't worry. Let Mary be.
She has chosen to sit and listen—
to be open to my Word. I am here only for a short while
so she has chosen well.
(and this is what Luke left out....)

But dear one, you know my Work is love.
Let me say to you
it is done not only in the great acts,
the heroic acts, the ones that bring notice,
but also plate by plate
and cup by cup."

The men shifted a little uneasily,
Mary raised her perfectly arched eyebrows,
and Martha, clapping her sudsy
thick chapped hands together,

cried "Amen!"

Rosie

Like a leaf that has fallen from the tree begins
to slowly curl in upon itself   away from the earth
she lies in the white hospital bed that has been
lowered close to the ground.
She'd been going back to the motherwomb for years now
bit by bit
a slow crawl toward that point
or that place before consciousness
before quickening.
Now she is almost there.

Who are you? she would ask her daughter daily
when she moved in with her some years ago in Maine.
I'm Karen.   You are my mother.
What a marvelous coincidence   her mother would say
that we find ourselves together here!

And later   after things stopped coming into focus for her the terrifying
closets of her childhood reopened.
Unmoored   she wheel knows what dark phantoms
down the nursing home hall home hall.
Now she was giving up even that strong
body that had held up through it all.

She has come back to that infant-place where you say
I wonder if she dreams? or   Do you think she hears us? and
Look, a smile!   the nurses carefully wiping the pap from her chin.

Her eyes are closed.   She is a curled leaf   her breath a rasp.
Hi Rosie   it's me Karen.   I'm here from Boston to see you.
Nothing.

She caresses her mother's hair   kisses her brow
strokes her thin arms.
And when there is no one looking   no nurses
no friend sitting by her side
she lifts the paper-soft eyelid to look inside
and sees just the reflection of herself
looking back in the black pupil.

A Response to Certain Postmodern Feminist Legal Scholars

We are our blood   or lack of it.
We   each one   must touch
those soft cotton grabbers of red
place and remove them
moon after moon
for forty years
stopped only by womb-fill
the spill turning into babes
or menopause.

No 'pollution' this
but terrifying power!
to bleed so
yet be so well.

Yes   yes   language does a structure make.
It puts its bricks around us.
I understand your chipping at the mortar
your tongue at the side of your mouth
teeth clenched
pushing back   or clipping off your hair
rebuilding with those old bricks
or throwing them out completely
mucking in the mud
looking for straw to make new stones.

Ah

but don't give up your woman eyes
betray your bodies' leaking selves.

Come back to magic   and to witchery
(where once we harnessed words
and rode them as we would).
Put womb and star dust in your clay.

Play if you will   on those jungle gyms
of abstract thought   your breasts a-jiggling
but then come down and plant your feet
against the earth from which you sprung

and let your construct sing a ruby song!

Grace

She sits on a spread checkered cloth
playing with a silken string
weaving it into the shaggy nest
where waves of her hair used to be.

She is drunk with how big
and how little 'things' are—
ants   sky   the roots of plants
dust.

She sees as clearly the space around
what is solid
as what it contains
as if it holds its own shape
and meaning.

Yesterday was her birthday
the one they said she wouldn't reach.
The Hooded One   caught   held back for now

by her will
which is as patient   complex
and reasonable
as a spider's web.

Blackbirds solemnly stroll like undertakers
in the grass.

She smiles
lifts her hand
blesses them.

Poem for Simonetta

I look at the frying pans in Marshalls.
I have a great large cast iron one and a small cast iron one
each encased in 50 years of carbon
beloved in their hold and heft.
But I need a 10 inch one.
I see the pans hanging from the hooks—
Cuisinart, Calphalon, T-Fal…
 I study the outsides, the insides,
their prices
and then I see it—

Per una cucina sana senza grazzi
fabrique en italie

and I think "Simonetta!"
Simonetta who I love
Simonetta who loves to cook
Simonetta my wild Italian friend.

It is beautiful—
a red the dark side of ruby
the sides of the bowl not too curved
not too straight
the black inside slightly bumpy…

I buy it.
I think "This will be my song to her".
I will think of her each time I use it.
I will ignore the "senza grassi"
and use Colivita olive oil and the best of butter.

For there is no better song
than the song we sing
the silent song deep inside
as we stir the eggs, brown the meat,
sauté the beans…
lift from pan onto plate—

the gift of food,
the gift of life.

Josephine

The color yellow
appears to advance,
creeping over the maples, the oaks.

When was it that my eyes turned milky?
When did these hands begin
to curl and shake,
these feet falter
under the weight of my
bird-boned body?
When did words become
dark fluttery things—
caved and hidden.

My neighbor Joe said, when he brought in my logs,
Looks like Spring is just around the corner.
Spring. I'm too old for it
with its shout of daffodils,
its whine of violets.
Winter calms me—white,
the lace of trees,
a cardinal here and there—
bright bows on black limbs.

The children, the children's children, all grown.
They say Come for Sunday dinner.
but I like my chair for drifting off
and the steady spread and purr of Theodore.

I listen to nothing
so much as the sound of nothing.
Summon scenes—
a young girl skipping rope,
an infant hand pressing on a breast,
the slap of a wave against bare skin...

The yellow will turn to gold
then rust again
until crows wing home,
cawing back the ink of night.

Sister Pat

Sister Pat kneels down
her arthritic knees scooping
the brown cushioned board.

She is waiting to hear the voice of her God.

Her dress is drab and muted
but the colors of the stained glass windows
touch her gently like a lover.

Her hands fold over one another.
Her knuckles are like rosary beads,
she could use them to count
her Aves and her Paters.

A memory of a young girl with long hair,
the feel of feet slapping across the dance floor
flits though her mind.

She has spent her life here—
these perfectly polished wood floors,
the precise writing on the blackboard,
the paired eyes of the little ones
taking her in…

There is no one to either side of her.
She is completely alone.

The medieval habit
abandoned some time ago
had made her magical
and mysterious and lovely.

Now she is just
another old woman in her 70's
empty as can be,
waiting to be filled.

"Hello, Pat" says God.

She smiles.

Elegy for Anne

I remember how you came on "the Ward"—
you, ripe 14, in yellow paper slippers
from some hospital that couldn't handle you,
the other kids in their Nikes, their Reeboks, sneering,
you shuffling, glaring at them, at me—
I loved you from the start.

I remember how the smoke-grey kitten
I gave you when you went into residential
climbed into your mother's clothes dryer to nap…
Her mind was on other things.

I remember how you grew into
the fullness of your beauty—
Italian-dark and curved like well-carved wood.
Men were bad to you. One locked you
in a house for a month in another country.
You got away.

I remember how I sat with you
while labor grabbed you in its fist.
How the cheeks of baby Mark
were squeezed by his father,
leaving two bruises like Lenten ashes
and DSS opened a case on you.
And how, fifteen years later
they took him away—
you in a vodka haze, promising to be good.

I remember how they found you at 39,
dead in your apartment in the projects—
your telephone disconnected, your cell phone unpaid,
the wires inside your head having stormed,
flashed, once again thrown you into spasms,
seized you off the couch, but this time,
no way to call for help.

But listen, Annie, I remember too
me taking you and Mark to Bugaboo's—
you pretending it was your birthday to get free cake,
a faint smell of liquor and cigarettes
on your breath, us laughing,
talking about what next good thing might come.

Portugal

We ride the ribbon road,
the land diving
like a tern to the sea.

We stop somewhere Ticha remembers—
a childhood swim spot
where the ocean is languid,
beguiled by the scent of eucalyptus.
She and Sharon swim and I,
coming down with something,
sit on the shore
saying over and over again in my head
the word for olives (ah-zay-toon-ahsh)
because it is so beautiful.
Later in the day we stand inside
the ruin of some perfect Roman thing—
temple or forum
that is now in the middle of nowhere.

And then, the Evora chapel—
a chapel made of bones.
Their smell—over powering yet familiar.
They are stacked, not sideways like a log cabin,
but densely side by side,
the knobby ends forming the walls.
Clusters of skulls make the arches,
and the long braids of centuries-dead women
hang before glass-eyed statues—
a sacrifice for the safe-come-home
of their beloveds.

Before leaving the town we eat bean soup
so good I actually cry.
I'm feverish now,
taking strange big pills from the farmacia.
We roll past the peeled cork

and the symmetrically placed olive trees—
back to Lisbon where notes of plaintive fados
drift among Moorish tiles and caged birds
call the alfama back to itself.

Standin' By

Sweet Jesus
Lizzie moans

they say he killed
that poor old woman
left the print of his ten tips
on the crocheted lace
she tatted herself
on the lace
of the pale pillowslip
he held over her face
til she stopped thrashing
til her chest
was as still
as stone

mercy!

I raised him right
at night I gave him honey
in his milk
did sums with him
on Sundays sent him pretty
 off to Bible class

for 10 dollars
in a purple Chevas purse
sang him *Summertime*
and danced him
up and down the floor

but demon drugs

ain't nothin' can harm you

grabbed mind and bone

lord

and now grey stone and steel
encase him in their empty arms

Women's March Boston
January 21, 2017

Standing on the crowded T
I see a woman look up. *I know you,* she says
Maggie Blanchard! I cry.
Fourteen years since,
we talk of the old times at "the Welfare",
of the recent funerals of those we worked with.
We are somehow there and here
at the same time.
Two women in their seventies
who went to jail for demonstrating in the sixties.
Now here and there.

Coming out of Park Street Station,
my daughter has lost her glove
It is a fancy and expensive glove—
warm with a fur cuff. She is slightly bereft.
We double back. It is nowhere.

We join the wave upon wave of those who have gathered—
side by side, knitted pink hats, a bobbing of brilliant
and witty signs. Songs, speeches.
The Common, every inch covered with people—
one hundred seventy-five thousand strong.

We have been standing for hours. We are tired.
We decide to leave after the rally
and skip the march part.
As we are leaving, two very small girls
impossibly dressed in the exact
same princess costume
come upon one another.
Let's dance! says the one.
And they do.

As we near the station's entry
I join my hands flat together
Please Saint Anthony, let me find that glove.
And then, surrounded by a large swath of grass,
it appears, that sister glove,
untrodden, pristine, waiting...
and all and anything
seems wonderful and possible.

Carol Siemering has been writing poetry for 70 years. She has been published in many different venues over those years including the *Catholic Worker* newspaper, the *Blue Collar Review,* an Anthology of Unitarian Universalist Poets, *The Artwork Quarterly, Unlocking the Poem, Fish Drum Poetry,* the liner notes of the *Grail Women in Chant and Harmony CD,* and the *Ekphrastic Review.* She lives in Newton, Massachusetts.

www.ingramcontent.com/pod-product-compliance
Lightning Source LLC
Chambersburg PA
CBHW022103080426
42734CB00009B/1477